The Word Wall

Teaching Vocabulary Through Immersion

JOSEPH GREEN

Pippin Publishing

Copyright © 2003 by Pippin Publishing Corporation
Suite 232
85 Ellesmere Road
Toronto
Ontario M1R 4B9

We acknowledge the financial support of the Government of
Canada through the Book Publishing Industry Development
Program for our publishing activities.
We acknowledge the support of the Government of Ontario
through the Ontario Media Development Corporation's Ontario
Book Initiative

Designed by John Zehethofer
Edited by Sylvia Hill
Typeset by Jay Tee Graphics Ltd.
Printed and bound in Canada by AGMV Marquis Imprimeur Inc.

National Library of Canada Cataloguing in Publication

Green, Joseph
    The word wall: teaching vocabulary through immersion / Joseph
Green. -- 2nd ed.

(The Pippin teacher's library ; 40)
ISBN 0-88751-110-4

    1. Language arts (Elementary) 2. Language arts (Secondary)
3. Vocabulary--Study and teaching (Elementary) 4. Vocabulary--
Study and teaching (Secondary) I. Title. II. Series: Pippin teacher's
library 40.

LB1576.G74 2003   372.6'044   C2003-903879-3

ISBN 0-88751-110-4

10 9 8 7 6 5 4 3 2 1

CONTENTS

. . . .

INTRODUCTION

Nothing gives birth to new ideas quite like desperation, and desperation is what I felt in the fall of 1975 when I was pulled from a sixth grade classroom in the affluent Pacific Heights district of San Francisco and placed into an ESEA Title 1* position in a school that was so different from my previous one it might well have been on the other side of the world. I was being stroked, my administration told me. My expertise in the classroom was being recognized and my skills were being given an appropriate arena of application that would fully prove their worth. I was ecstatic! I was inspired! I was totally out of touch with reality.

In the previous three years my Pacific Heights kids had demanded that I excel. Bright and self-motivated, they had come to me with above grade-level reading skills, superb math abilities, and a drive to learn that made it clear to me from my first day in the classroom with them that they were watching me closely. For these children the school year was like a marathon foot-race. They were not looking for exercise. Each wanted to be the first to break the tape, and if I wasn't going to assist in that effort then they had little use for me.

* For those unfamiliar with U.S. educational terminology, ESEA stands for The Elementary and Secondary Education Act. It is a federally funded act of Congress, designed to address that portion of the country's student population in grades one through twelve which falls below the fiftieth percentile in reading and/or language skills as indicated by scores on nationally normed standardized tests. (The term *Title 1* merely indicates the source of the monies which has been identified for this purpose in the federal budget.) The total amount allocated to each school is based upon a per student expenditure formula, so the budget will vary from year to year depending upon the number of qualifying students. The money covers the placement of one full-time teacher and one paraprofessional, with a budget for materials and supplies. It is intended to supplement the efforts of the classroom teacher by providing small-group tutorial assistance to those students deemed to be at risk of failure.

A compensatory education program, its stated goal is to work itself out of existence by eliminating the need for such services.

Steven argued ethics with me, citing Hegel and Spinoza as referents. Tyler was a mathematical prodigy who wrote papers investigating the axiomatic principles governing finite numbers. She expected me not only to understand her arguments but to comment upon them. And Peter, whose father was a doctor, knew more about the human body than did most pre-med students.

Persuading them to read was not the problem. They ate up the standard, district-required basal series before the winter break, seasoning their consumption of it with enough venom and degradation to qualify it as a dangerous substance with the U.S. Environmental Protection Agency. Exhortations from me that this form of intellectual sustenance was vital for their over-all development as students was met with derisive laughter. Offering them a reading program for the gifted, in a futile attempt to assuage their anger, only served to move me from being an object of ridicule to a target for verbal assault. We finally negotiated a settlement that found its center in a teacher-directed reading list based on their individual interests, with concessions made for good literature. So began what was to be my only truly collaborative experience in a classroom setting.

This experience was a teacher's dream come true, though I had little real appreciation of the true extent of my good fortune until I plunged through that academic stratosphere and landed with a thump at my new school.

The kids in Pacific Heights had dared me to keep up with them. The children before me now were the spectators of education. They stood on the sidelines and dreamed of catching the big one even while they jeered at those who did. Lunch and recess were the high points of their school day, and the dare they offered me was that of defiant disorder. "Get to me," they were saying with their contempt. "Get me out of the stands and into the game, only don't make it look like that's what I've always wanted anyway."

My time at Pacific Heights had been spent with champions. My role had been ladder-builder, with the only dare I confronted that to my own pride. Now I found myself facing the other end of the spectrum. These students had no obvious goals at all. Not only were they not reaching for the sky, they seemed not even to know the sky was there.

It quickly became apparent to me that I needed a curriculum

that caught them looking the other way while I sneakily taught them something. I was certain that these kids needed form and structure if they were to grow academically stronger: they were convinced that if learning wasn't fun, then learning wasn't worth their time or effort.

They had done their basal thing and it had left them wanting. Their basal readers filled their cumulative record folders; creatively conceived comic books were wonderfully colored in but evidently unread.

The ESEA Title 1 teacher who had preceded me (and fled screaming from the building six weeks earlier) had operated almost exclusively in the affective domain, and the room was filled with the paraphernalia associated with this approach. These materials were in various states of use ranging from untouched to completely destroyed, and it was obvious that they had had little effect on this tough crew. My only advantage over these kids was that at least I knew what had not worked for them. My challenge now was to come up with materials that would motivate them and survive their assault; so I retreated to the unknown comfort of the curriculum catalogs that fill every teacher's mailbox in search of that magic academic ingredient.

Convinced that some item in these catalogs was just what I was looking for, I pored over them whenever I had a spare moment. I was equally convinced that anything with the slightest resemblance to normal classroom fare did not stand a chance of succeeding; so I stretched my criteria for acceptable materials well beyond what would normally be considered educationally prudent. I quickly depleted the small budget allocated to me for such acquisitions, and mounds of "good stuff" soon filled my room from the floor to ceiling.

Each item held a diamond hidden somewhere in it; each item was implemented with as much enthusiasm as I could project. Some materials caught the kids' attention immediately, involved them completely for a few brief days, and then were ignored. Some materials were worked at grudgingly and slowly as if to fulfil a sentence incurred by the commission of some unknown wrongdoing, and some materials were rejected outright as being babyish or silly.

The "good stuff" became just so much clutter to be boxed up and shared with my colleagues who loved to get my cast-offs. Each time I retired one of those clever ideas that hadn't quite made it, it became more obvious to me that I was on the ropes with these kids. I was accomplishing nothing. Then, one day, while I was watching at recess, I noticed something that should have been obvious to me many months earlier. As losers for most of their short lives, winning was what they wanted more than anything else. Competition was their motivation and it didn't seem to matter how it came dressed: Foot races, kickball, basketball, even fistfights gave them the opportunity to feel like winners at something. Competition, I decided, was what I too needed to provide in the classroom. If I were to have any chance at all of reaching them, I needed something that would link competition to the reading skills they so desperately needed. I needed materials that would make these kids want to invest themselves in the process of becoming better readers, and such materials, as I knew from my many hours spent with catalogs, did not exist anywhere in the realm of published curriculum. These materials, I now knew, would of necessity have to come from my own mind.

* * *

Years ago, while teaching at an experimental school in a different city, I had had a marginally insane idea for a semi-functional room decoration. I have always been reluctant to use my classroom as a showpiece for parents and administrators, and have resisted the standard elementary school practice of changing the décor of my room with the passage of seasons. I prefer my room to be a workspace rather than a showroom. This attitude was not well accepted by either parents or administrators and as a way around their criticism, I devised the following: Using the "Dale List of the Most Commonly Used Words in English" and a touch of Gestalt psychology, I filled the walls of my room with words printed on tagboard strips and cut to highlight the differences in word shapes. I referred to it as a "word-immersion" technique when questioned about it by administrators, parents, or colleagues. I was, therefore, surprised when my word decoration became much more than that with little effort on my part.

The word-festooned walls were ignored for the first few months of their life and appeared to be nothing more than what they were intended to be — decorative. But that was before I inserted the Free-Time Block into the schoolday. (A Free-Time Block was introduced when I was certain that the group I was

4

working with could handle unstructured time productively.) The room took on a different tone and form during these periods, becoming almost completely student-centered and ostensibly not directed toward academic goals. Games, art projects, comic books, manipulatives, and other non-school related activities appeared from their closeted exile and held dominion over the classroom for the last thirty minutes of the day.

Students who had been assigned to peer groups earlier in the school year would team up for a rousing game of UNO, WAR, or even Blackjack. Others would go to their desks for a teacher-made game of concentration, and a few would retreat to the back of the room for a checkers or chess game. What they did was of their own choosing as long as they did nothing to disturb other groups. This plan had worked well in preceding years with the children enjoying the activities as much as they did the opportunity of planning and executing a part of their own day. They seldom did anything to cause me to end this free time and return them to more predictable classroom activities, but that was before the advent of the decorative "word-immersion" technique. After a period of undetectable perception (a technique often used by this grade-level student to guard against the possibility of having to admit that the teacher actually had a good idea), pairs of children began to exhibit a strange behavior.

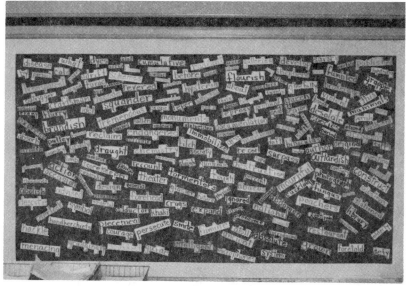

Portion of the Orange Word Wall

Positioning themselves in front of one of the word-decorated walls, they invented a competition. One student would stand before the wall; the other would sit on the floor or in a chair near that wall. The standing student would point to words on the wall and the sitting student would say each word, continuing to do so until missing a word, at which the students traded places. Often a third child became involved as a scorekeeper, and they rotated roles. Unfortunately, more often than not, chaos would ensue as each child vied for dominance by exhibiting mastery of a particular wall.

Beginning with only a few children, this game was soon adopted by many others and the Free-Time Block turned into a word-wall game period for all but a few students. Although their game fitted most of the criteria established for the Free-Time Block, it certainly did not meet the requirement that the activity not disturb other groups. Those few students who chose to remain uninvolved were definitely being disturbed. The teacher in me loved to see children voluntarily engaged in academic behavior but the disciplinarian and classroom manager in me soon realized that this behavior could not go unchecked. So the word walls were removed as an option during the Free-Time Block. That did not stop the activity; it merely drove it underground. Pairs of children began whispering the words to each other while still in their seats.

"It begins with a **d**, ends with a **t** and rhymes with *pot*," one would say to the other. Or: "It's written in red, has an **ou** in the middle, and means the same thing as *tough*." The walls seemed to call to them and they even risked censure from me to play this game. Why they did this seemed obvious to me. They were children: prohibition breeds desire in the very young. What they can't have, they want the most; and what they are forbidden to have, they want the most of all. They thought they were getting away with something, I decided, and the best way to extinguish that belief was to give them what they thought they were taking. *The Word Wall* would no longer be off limits. It would become part of the week's curriculum. That would stop this foolishness! Once it became work, *The Word Wall*'s charm would quickly fade.

Taking my lead from the children, I worked up a script similar to the ones I knew they were using.

"Find a word," I wrote, "that begins with an **l**, ends with a **g**, and rhymes with *sung*." "Find a word that begins with an **s**, ends with a **t** and has a /kr/* sound in the middle." This first list contained only ten words; the clues were almost totally phonetic, and the activity was plugged in at the end of a reading lesson as a filler. I gave the filler about a week's lifespan, believing that once it became required it would quickly expire. Near riot faced me at the end of that first session. They demanded to know why there were only ten lousy words.

Student identifying a word

In the following weeks the filler activity grew to twenty words with a phonetic base, then to words with phonetic and structural clues, and then to phonetic, structural, and contextual clues. *The Word Wall* became an integral part of the classroom curriculum valued by everyone.

Drawing on word summaries and vocabulary lists from their standard readers, the word lists increased. Levels of difficulty were built into each wall using grade-level proficiency standards. Adjectives, antonyms, synonms, homonyms, and even exonyms — words borrowed from other languages — were given space on the walls and clues in the guide I was developing. The procedural aspects of play became more sophisticated. The list of possible applications for *The Word Wall* grew with every use

---

* The diacritical markings / / relate to the *sound(s)* a leter or letters stand for or represent. For example, the letters **cr** stand for the /kr/ sound. The letters **ou** can stand for the sound heard in *rough*.

and the greater its scope became, the more the children enjoyed themselves. Ten o'clock Friday morning became the highpoint of the week and the very worst thing that could happen for these children was to miss *The Word Wall* period.

The Word Wall was, therefore, where I turned when I finally realized that this was the competitive element needed by children to succeed. *The Word Wall* proved to be the competitive lure that drew these ''spectators'' of education out of the stands and into the game.

Three months later, while still below grade level, all but three of my students showed a minimum growth of O.8 (eight months) in their total reading scores on the California Test of Basic Skills. A year later only one child tested more than five months below grade level. But the most telling of all evaluations was given by their classroom teachers who, without exception, reported that these children had shown a significant increase in their desire to learn. They were back in the game.

The Word Wall became an integral part of my classroom with that group of children: it has remained an integral part of my teaching for the last fifteen years with comparable results. It has been used in urban and suburban areas, and has been successful in inner city schools as well as affluent neighborhood schools. It has challenged bright and involved students and motivated the reluctant learner. Its applications have increased with each year of use and it remains today, as yesterday, one of the high points of my students' week. A room decoration turned curriculum, *The World Wall* has proven its worth many times over.

Students playing Word Wall

. . . .

THE PROCESS

W hat, then, is this thing called *The Word Wall*? What piece of classroom curriculum could possibly stand up to the claims made for it? It is, quite simply, exactly what it appears to be — a set of six word-filled panels, each with a different background color, each with a different goal. It can be used to teach phonic elements, word form classes, grammatical forms, and spelling patterns, but its prime objective is the development of vocabulary skills. All of its other applications are predicated on the belief that efficient reading is the cumulative result of the development of a broad matrix of skills, each of which is necessary before vocabulary acquisition can occur. The range of *The Word Wall*'s utility has, therefore, been broadened with each year's use to incorporate as many of these component parts as is possible without losing sight of the target.

Almost subliminal in its effect upon students *The Word Wall*, when used as prescribed, is a powerful learning tool that can be added easily to any classroom management system with positive results. It has proved effective in small group remedial and developmental applications, peer-pairing arrangements, whole classroom instruction modes, and with individual students.

Never stored on a shelf or hidden away in a desk, *The Word Wall* naturally becomes part of the room relatively quickly. Students use it independently as a thesaurus and spell-check program during writing assignments; they use it as a resource during language development lessons, and often choose *The Word Wall* as an activity during rainy-day lunch periods or recesses. Its most efficient use, however, is in the standard classroom setting, and the instructions that follow are, therefore, directed toward its use in that environment.

1: Student Involvement

The required first step is to provide student motivation. This is best accomplished through the establishment of teams because of the game orientation underwritten in the use of *The Word Wall*. In the initial stage it is competition that drives the learning process. Team assignment can be accomplished in a number of ways ranging from random count-off procedures to student selection of members. A word of caution: For at least the first quarter of the school year, team parity is an essential element of class division. Each team must reflect the range of abilities present in every classroom to prevent domination by a single team. If this balance does not exist, the dominated teams soon cease to be fully involved. It is, therefore, recommended that you choose the teams initially through the use of standardized test scores or some other empirically validated source of information. Teams should be changed at least once during the course of the year, at which time other methods of selection can be used.

Once teams are selected and named (an essential for elementary students), the Rules of Play (see pages 13-15), must be carefully explained. Classroom management problems will arise if this instructional component is not explained comprehensively, and the learning process is reduced. Before each game, explain the Rules of Play thoroughly. Students should have at least two "dry run" games during which scores are not entered to ensure that the procedures are firmly in the minds of students.

2: Integration with the Curriculum

The Word Wall is most effective when it is perceived by your students as a regular and predictable part of classroom activities. It should, therefore, become a physical part of your room prior to the opening of a school term and an instructional part no later than the third or fourth week of that term. It must then be played at least once a week and the day and time of play should not vary.

Regular use is essential for the success of the program because it provides two important elements in the education of elementary school students: predictability and repetition. *The Word Wall* will be of little value if it ignores these two essentials. Your students need to know that you value *The Word Wall* enough to repeat it weekly. It, and the skills it is designed to teach, then become significant in the minds of your students.

In addition, *The Word Wall* is built upon the spiral theory of mastery — repetition reinforces previously learned principles. Regular use throughout the school year allows you to recycle many words and the skills attendant on them through the minds of your students, thus ensuring greater retention.

A clearly displayed bar graph that records each team's victories helps to keep students involved by maintaining the competitive element of *The Word Wall*'s game orientation. When I use it, I also promise tangible rewards for the winning team, a ploy that helps to promote teamwork but does not detract from the learning experience. Students' teamwork in this area often transfers to other classroom activities, and can sometimes lead to co-operative learning experiences initiated solely by the students.

Note: In my classes the reward is an ice-cream and cookie party at the end of each quarter of the school year. In the fifteen-year history of *The Word Wall* in my classroom no winning team has ever refused to share their spoils with their vanquished classmates.

3: *Specific Lesson Plans*

Your class will likely remind you what day it is and what usually happens on that day, but it is still preferable for teaching purposes to build *The Word Wall* into a specific lesson plan with a pre-identified list of words for that week for which reinforcement activities can be constructed. *The Word Wall* is effective on its own in both motivational and operational roles but it is not meant to be a cumulative activity in and of itself. The game begins the learning process. The game introduces the words, gives them meaning beyond sound alone, and welds form to function, but it is the follow-up activities that allow students to use those words introduced to them by *The Word Wall* in a meaningful context that complete the learning process. Suggestions for contextual activities follow the itemized word lists. These activities are only exemplary in nature and will, of necessity, have to be individually designed to meet the needs of the user group. However, it is their use that will finally close the circle and give full learning value to the process.

The Rules of Play, as described on pages 13-15, provide the essential operational skeleton for the activity. They have been designed to be straightforward, direct, and uncomplicated. If followed carefully they facilitate word awareness, spelling patterns, phonic elements, and vocabulary development.

4: Role of Teacher

Your role is best described as that of a benevolent dictator: it is a role similar to that of a referee in an athletic event where you act as the mediating force between teams who are motivated primarily by the desire to win, with you maintaining absolute control. Your decisions are final. If argument from participants is permitted, it will inevitably detract from the overall effectiveness of the exercise. You must, therefore, make it quite clear from the outset that you are the final arbiter of all disputes.

Acting as arbiter/referee, you will have to make judgment calls on which student's hand is raised first. When the choice is between a consistently motivated student and a hitherto reluctant, non-participating student, it is obviously politically expedient to encourage the reluctant student. Such behavior on your part will not create resentment among the players; often, these players will follow your example and praise the reluctant players, which encourages them to continue being involved.

When the Bonus Point stage of *The Word Wall* is reached, you must again exercise some judgment. If the continued involvement of a player is at risk because misspellings exceed the limit as defined by the rules, then it is advisable not to hold that student to the same standards as those imposed on the majority.

RULES OF PLAY

The following script has proven to be most effective establishing the Rules of Play.

1. The object of this game is for one of two teams to get more points than the opposing team. This is done by finding the most words on the Word Walls by using the clues I give you.

2. As you can see, there are six Word Walls, each with a different background color. I identify the wall on which you will find the word by its color. I begin each clue by saying:
   Find the word on the (red, blue, green, yellow, white, or orange) wall.
   To be certain that you know which wall we will be using each time I give clues, please point to the walls as I name them.
   a. Point to the Red Wall.
   b. Point to the Blue Wall.
   c. Point to the Green Wall.
   d. Point to the Yellow Wall.
   e. Point to the Orange Wall.
   f. Point to the White Wall.

3. I will then give you one of these clue patterns:
   a. Find the *complete* word on the Red Wall. (SIGHT ONLY — *parenthetical elements are for your information. They define the skill(s) students employ to find the word.*)
   b. Find the word on the Blue Wall that rhymes with *seat*. (SOUND ONLY)
   *c. Find the word on the White Wall with a beginning

---

* The diacritical markings / / relate to the *sound(s)* a letter or letters stand for or represent. For example, the letter **b** stands for the /b/ sound. The letters **oa** stand for the ō sound. The mark above the ō represents the long (free) sound.

sound /b/, a middle sound /ō/ with an **oa** pattern, an ending sound /t/, and which names something we use to float on a lake. (SOUND AND MEANING)

d. Find the word on the White Wall with a beginning sound /sh/, a middle sound /ā/ because of the silent **e** at the end, an ending sound /v/, and which fits into the following sentence: 'My father has to _____ his beard every morning. (SOUND AND CONTEXT)

e. Find the word on the Green Wall with the prefix **re**, a middle sound /ē/ made with an **ea** pattern, an ending sound /d/, and which means to read again. (SOUND, MEANING, STRUCTURE)

f. Find the word on the Red Wall with a beginning sound /h/, a middle sound /ū/ because of the silent **e** at the end, an ending sound /j/ made with **ge** pattern, and which is an adjective I might use to describe an elephant. (SOUND, MEANING, CLASS)

Note: *At this point the goal of each clue is limited only by student need and your creativity. Using the forms above, any number of personalized clues can be devised.*

4. It is very important that I complete the entire clue before you raise your hands, so wait until I have stopped completely even if you find the word during the sound clues. Game points will be taken from your team if hands are raised before I have completed the clue.

5. Once I have completed the clue and you have found the word, raise your hands to announce that you know where the word is to be found. I will call on the student whose hand goes up first. In case of a tie the "Three-Count Rule" will be used to break the tie.

6. When we need to use the "Three-Count Rule," these steps are followed:

a. Students who are tied place their hands flat on their desktops. I then count to three and the first hand to go up when I say *three* wins the tie and goes to the Wall. If we have three consecutive ties during the "three-count" tie-breaker, a coin flip decides who goes to the wall.

7. The student who raises his or her hand first or who breaks the tie then goes to the wall on which the word is found and, using a pointer, identifies the word. The student must go directly to the word. Once at the wall, no further searching will be permitted.

8. After the student points out the word he or she must then say it directly. Three chances are given to accomplish this. If that student fails, the ''Three-Count Rule'' is used to pick another student to say the word. That student gets only one chance to say the word because the handraising has told us that he or she already knows how to say the word.

   If the student who finds the word says it correctly, his or her team gets the point. If the student chosen by the ''Three-Count Rule'' says the word correctly, then his or her team gets the point. If no one can find the word, or if once it has been found no one can say it, then no points are given; I say the word and you all write it in your Word Wall Journals.

9. Once the word has been found and said, all of you write it on your Student Response Sheet and I go on to the next word.

Note: *The Student Response Sheet has the student's name and date, and can be pre-numbered for writing each word that is on your list for the specific match.*

10. Once all the words on my list have been found, you have three minutes to check your spellings. I will then check your papers. Each of you is allowed one ''free'' misspelling for which no team points will be deducted, but every misspelling after that will cause your team to lose a point. If everyone on your team produces a perfect list, then your team will receive five extra bonus points.

11. The team with the most points after the spelling check wins the match.

A WORD WALL BLUEPRINT

The eight Word Lists, and the accompanying Reinforcement and Evaluation Activities that follow are primers only. They are applicable to classroom settings as they stand and can be productively implemented. However, they only begin the process of making *The Word Wall* a permanent part of your classroom. These lists are the blueprints for you to construct succeeding lists, and exercises. Each class will use *The Word Wall* in a slightly different fashion and, once you have begun to apply it to your particular situation, the direction indicated by students' needs will be obvious.

The format of your approach to each item is, however, basically the same.

WORD LIST 1: GENERAL REVIEW

This list of twenty-five words is the first list used during the school year. The words contained in the list cover grade levels from first to eighth, and almost all of the suggested script forms are introduced within it. Use this list for the "dry run" games mentioned under the heading *Student Involvement*, page 10. Do not hesitate to use it in both the first and second sessions. Familiarity with it in the second presentation allows for refinement of procedure.

1. PHONICS/STRUCTURE/
   MEANING
   YELLOW WALL

   download

   Find the word on the Yellow Wall that is a compound word that begins with a /d/ sound, has an /l/ sound in the middle, ends with a /d/ sound and means "to install information on your computer from the Internet."

2. SIGHT
   GREEN WALL

   smart

   Find the word *smart* on the Green Wall.

3. PHONICS/STRUCTURE/
   MEANING
   GREEN WALL

   reset

   Find the word on the Green Wall that begins with the prefix **r e**, ends with the small word "set" and means "to begin again."

4. PHONICS/MEANING
   ORANGE WALL

   Find the word on the Orange Wall with a beginning sound

foolish

/f/, a middle sound /oo/, an ending sound of /ĭsh/ and which means the same as "silly."

5. PHONICS/STRUCTURE/
MEANING
YELLOW WALL

hardcopy

Find the compound word on the Yellow Wall that begins with an /h/ sound, has a /k/ sound in the middle made with a **c o** pattern, ends with a /pee/ sound made with a **p y** pattern, and names what we get when we print out a computer file.

6. PHONICS/MEANING
YELLOW WALL

quarter

Find the word on the Yellow Wall with a beginning sound /kw/, a middle sound /or/, an ending sound /er/, and which names a coin worth 25 cents.

7. PHONICS/MEANING
ORANGE WALL

quality

Find the word on the Orange Wall that begins with a /qu/ sound, has an /l/ sound in the middle, ends with a /tee/ sound made with a **t y** pattern, and means "the very best."

8. PHONICS/MEANING
YELLOW WALL

scales

Find a word on the Yellow Wall with a beginning sound /sk/ made with an **s c** pattern, a middle sound /ā/ because of a silent **e**, an ending sound /z/ made with an **s**, and which names a part of a fish's body.

9. PHONICS/SIGHT
YELLOW WALL

herbivore

Find a word on the Yellow Wall with a silent **h** at the beginning of it. Find the word *herbivore*.

10. PHONICS/MEANING
ORANGE WALL

apology

Find the word on the Orange Wall with a beginning sound /ā/, a middle sound /1/, an ending sound /gē/ with a **g y** pattern, and which names what you say to a person when you say that you are sorry.

11. PHONICS/MEANING
    GREEN WALL

    burrow

Find the word on the Green Wall with a beginning sound /b/, a middle sound /ur/, an ending sound /ō/ made with an **o w** pattern, and which names the tunnels some small animals live in.

12. PHONICS/STRUCTURE/
    MEANING
    GREEN WALL

    policeman

Find a compound word on the Green Wall with a beginning sound /p/, a middle sound /s/ made with a **c e** pattern, an ending sound /n/, and which names a person who protects us from criminals.

13. PHONICS/MEANING
    GREEN WALL

    giant

Find the word on the Green Wall with a beginning sound /j/ made with a **g**, a middle sound /ă/, an ending sound /t/, and which is an opposite of the word *midget*.

14. PHONICS/STRUCTURE/
    MEANING
    ORANGE WALL

    successful

Find the word on the Orange Wall with a beginning sound /s/, a middle sound /s/ made with a **c**, ending with the suffix **ful**, and which is an opposite of the word *failure*.

15. SIGHT
    ORANGE WALL

    domesticate

Find the word *domesticate* on the Orange Wall.

16. PHONICS/CONTEXT
    YELLOW WALL

    recognize

Find the word on the Yellow Wall with a beginning sound /r/, a middle sound /k/ made with a **c**, an ending sound /z/, and which fits into this sentence: He did not _____ the stranger; so he would not get close to his car.

19

17. PHONICS/MEANING
    YELLOW WALL

    complete

Find the word on the Yellow Wall with a beginning sound /k/, a middle sound /ē/ because of a silent **e*** at the end, a final sound /t/, and which means to finish something you've started.

18. PHONICS/MEANING
    ORANGE WALL

    comfortable

Find the word on the Orange Wall with a beginning sound /k/ made with a **c**, a middle sound /f/, an ending sound /əbəl/, and which means the same as the word *relaxed*.

19. SIGHT
    YELLOW WALL

    relationship

Find the word *relationship* on the Yellow Wall.

20. PHONICS/MEANING
    YELLOW WALL

    hundred

Find the word on the Green Wall with a beginning sound /h/, a middle sound /dr/, an ending sound /d/, and which names the number after *ninety-nine*.

21. PHONICS/STRUCTURE
    ORANGE WALL

    limestone

Find the compound word on the Orange Wall with a beginning sound /l/, a middle sound /st/, an ending sound /n/, and which has two long vowel sounds* in it because of silent **es** at the end of the two words that make the compound word.

---

22. SIGHT
    YELLOW WALL

    enter

Find the word "enter" on the Yellow Wall.

23. SIGHT
    ORANGE WALL

    somersault

Find the word *somersault* on the Orange Wall.

24. PHONICS/MEANING
    ORANGE WALL

    vigor

Find the word on the Orange Wall with a beginning sound /v/, a middle sound /g/, an ending sound /ər/, and which means the same as the word *energy*.

25. STRUCTURE/MEANING
    GREEN WALL

    inside

Find the compound word on the Green Wall which is an opposite of the word *outside*.

WORD LIST 2: DOLCH FORMS

— INITIAL CONSONANTS

This list takes its direction from the Dolch List of phonic presentation and is the first to be used in the program. It provides a base upon which the other lists are built, though it is not in the purest sense a vocabulary development exercise. Contextual format is implemented as often as possible as are meaning clues, but decoding remains its primary focus.

The list uses only the first section of the Dolch List. Other word lists based on this one should be developed to address the remaining components of the Dolch List if students using the program require additional practice.

Note: The use of the term *consonant* can be dropped if you prefer. Sound/letter (phoneme/grapheme) correspondence need not be dependent on students' familiarity with additional labels if their basal readers do not embrace a phonic/decoding strand.

1. PHONICS/CONTEXT
   RED WALL

   business

   Find the word on the Red Wall with a beginning consonant sound /b/, an ending consonant sound /z/, and which fits into this sentence: I do not think that it is any of your _____.

2. PHONICS/CONTEXT
   WHITE WALL

   doughnut

   Find the word on the White Wall with a beginning consonant sound /d/, an ending consonant sound /t/, and which fits into this sentence: He ate the _____ with chocolate sprinkles on it.

3. PHONICS/SYNONYM
   ORANGE WALL

   foolish

Find the word on the Orange Wall with a beginning consonant sound /f/, an ending sound /sh/, and which means the same as the word *silly*.

4. PHONICS/MEANING
   GREEN WALL

   hungry

Find the word on the Green Wall with a beginning consonant sound /h/, an ending sound of /grē/, and which names how you feel when you want something to eat.

5. PHONICS/MEANING
   WHITE WALL

   junk

Find the word on the White Wall with a beginning consonant sound /j/, the ending consonant sound /k/, and which names something we throw away when we clean out our rooms.

6. PHONICS/MEANING
   WHITE WALL

   bicycle

Find the word on the White Wall with a beginning consonant sound /b/, an ending consonant sound /əl/ made with an **l e** pattern, and which names something with two-wheels and handlebars.

7. PHONICS/SYNONYM
   RED WALL

   dumb

Find the word on the Red Wall with a beginning consonant sound /d/, an ending consonant sound /m/, a silent **b** as the last letter, and which means the same thing as the word *stupid*.

8. PHONICS/MEANING
   GREEN WALL

   funny

Find the word on the Green Wall with a beginning consonant sound /f/, the ending sound /nē/ made with an **n y** pattern, and which names what we think something is when we laugh.

9. PHONICS/CONTEXT
RED WALL

hobbies

Find the word on the Red Wall with a beginning consonant sound /h/, an ending consonant sound /z/ made with **s**, and which fits into this sentence: Stamp collecting and stickers are _____ .

10. PHONICS/MEANING
RED WALL

juggler

Find the word on the Red Wall that has the same beginning consonant sound as the word *jump,* an ending sound /lər/, and which names a person who keeps a lot of things in the air at the same time.

11. PHONICS/CONTEXT
BLUE WALL

kettle

Find the word on the Blue Wall with a beginning consonant sound /k/, an ending consonant sound /l/, made with an **l e** pattern, and which fits into this sentence: Mom put the vegetables and water into a _____ and put it on the stove.

12. PHONICS/MEANING
BLUE WALL

lung

Find the word on the Blue Wall with a beginning consonant sound /l/, an ending consonant sound /g/, and which names the part of our body we use for breathing.

13. PHONICS/MEANING
BLUE WALL

March

Find the word on the Blue Wall with the same beginning consonant sound as the word *may,* the same ending consonant sound as the word *church,* and which names the month that follows February.

14. PHONICS/MEANING
GREEN WALL

knowledge

Find the word on the Green Wall that begins with an /n/ sound made with a **k n** pattern, has a silent **w** in the middle, ends with a /j/ sound made with a **g e** pattern, and means "things that we know about."

15. PHONICS/MEANING
    RED WALL

    pound

Find the word on the Red Wall with the same beginning consonant sound as the word *pack,* the same ending consonant sound as the word *band,* and which names what a person does with a hammer.

16. PHONICS/CONTEXT
    ORANGE WALL

    kind

Find the word on the Orange Wall with a beginning consonant sound /k/, an ending sound /d/, and which fits into this sentence: Grandpa is a very _____ and gentle man.

17. PHONICS/MEANING
    BLUE WALL

    laugh

Find the word on the Blue Wall with a beginning consonant sound /l/, an ending consonant sound /f/ made by a **g h** pattern, and which names what we do when we think something is funny.

18. PHONICS/MEANING
    WHITE WALL

    milk

Find the word on the White Wall with the same beginning consonant sound as the word *mouse,* the same ending consonant sound as the word *walk,* and which names a drink we get from cows.

19. PHONICS/MEANING
    RED WALL

    matrix

Find the word on the Red Wall that begins with an /m/ sound, has a /tr/ sound in the middle, ends with an /ix/ sound and means "a complex association among thoughts or ideas."

20. PHONICS/MEANING
    GREEN WALL

    poor

Find the word on the Green Wall that rhymes with *door,* and which names someone who does not have a lot of money.

21. PHONICS/ANTONYM
    BLUE WALL

    bottom

Find the word on the Blue Wall with a beginning consonant sound /b/, an ending consonant sound /m/, and which is the opposite of the word *top.*

22. PHONICS/CONTEXT
    WHITE WALL

    dent

Find the word on the White Wall with the same beginning consonant sound as the word *door,* the same ending consonant sound as the word *tent,* and which fits into this sentence: My Dad's car has a big _____ in the door.

23. PHONICS/MEANING
    RED WALL

    point

Find the word on the Red Wall that rhymes with *joint,* has a beginning consonant sound /p/, an ending consonant /t/, and which names what a pencil has when we sharpen it.

24. PHONICS/MEANING
    GREEN WALL

    neck

Find the word on the Green Wall with a beginning consonant sound /n/, an ending consonant sound /k/, and which names the part of your body your head sits on.

25. PHONICS/MEANING
    RED WALL

    fuse

Find the word on the Red Wall with the same beginning consonant sound as the word *fuss,* the same ending consonant sound as the word *lose,* and which names the part of a firecracker you light.

WORD LIST 3: GENERIC LIST EXEMPLAR

*T*he *Word Wall* is not always used to teach an exclusive element such as affixes. Quite often the list generated for use during a given week is purposely non-specific and covers a wide range of word classes and structural conversions. A goal of a word list might be that of reinforcement which, in keeping with the spiral format of *The Word Wall*, reinforces previously presented materials in the uncontrolled and more natural manner they would be encountered during the actual reading process.

This type of list might also be used to check for understanding and retention and, when that is the goal, your major concern is not to instruct but rather to assess.

This format for list construction is then the one that should be used when you are not concentrating on a specific area of study. It can encompass what has been previously taught either through *The Word Wall* or other methodologies. The most broadly useful list format, its placement at the beginning of the program is purposeful. It should be used repeatedly throughout the school year whenever you feel that reinforcement, review, or informal assessment is necessary.

1. SIGHT/MEANING
   WHITE WALL

   variable

   The word *variable* describes something that changes often. Find the word *variable* on the White Wall.

2. PHONICS/STRUCTURE
   BLUE WALL

   cowboy

   Find the compound word on the Blue Wall with a beginning sound /k/, a middle sound /b/, an ending sound /oy/ made with an **o y** pattern.

3. PHONICS/MEANING
   RED WALL

   huge

Find the word on the Red Wall with a beginning sound /h/, a middle sound /ū/ because of a silent **e** at the end, an ending sound /j/ made with a **g e** pattern, and which means extremely large.

4. PHONICS/STRUCTURE/
   MEANING
   BLUE WALL

   doubtful

Find the word on the Blue Wall with a beginning sound /d/, a silent **b** in the middle, ending with the suffix **ful**, and which means an uncertain feeling.

5. PHONICS/STRUCTURE/
   MEANING
   WHITE WALL

   crossroads

Find the compound word on the White Wall with a beginning sound /kr/ made with a **c r** pattern, a middle sound /r/, an ending sound /z/ made with an **s**, and which names a place where two streets or roads cross each other.

6. PHONICS/STRUCTURE/
   MEANING
   RED WALL

   recall

Find the word on the Red Wall beginning with the prefix **re**, a middle sound /k/ made with a **c**, an ending sound /l/, and which means the same as the word *remember*.

7. SIGHT/MEANING
   BLUE WALL
   sinister

Sinister is a synonym for the word *evil*. Find the word *sinister* on the Blue Wall.

8. PHONICS/STRUCTURE/
   MEANING
   WHITE WALL

   delightful

Find the word on the White Wall with a beginning sound /d/, a silent **g h** in the middle, ending with the suffix **ful**, and which means something that gives joy.

9. SIGHT/STRUCTURE
   RED WALL
   we've

Find the word on the Red Wall that is the contraction of ''we have.''

10. PHONICS/STRUCTURE/
    MEANING
    WHITE WALL

    defeat

Find the word on the White Wall with a beginning sound /d/, a middle sound /ē/ made with an **e a** pattern, an ending sound /t/, and which means to beat an opponent at a game.

11. PHONICS/STRUCTURE/
    MEANING
    WHITE WALL

    bicycle

Find the word on the White Wall beginning with the prefix **bi**, a middle sound /s/ made with a **c**, an ending sound /l/ made with an **l e** pattern, and which names a two-wheeled machine for riding on.

12. SIGHT
    BLUE WALL
       opportunity

Find the word *opportunity* on the Blue Wall.

13. PHONICS/STRUCTURE/
    MEANING
    WHITE WALL

    teacher

Find the word on the White Wall with a beginning sound /t/, a middle sound /ē/ made with an **e a** pattern, an ending sound /cher/, and which names what I am in a school.

14. PHONICS/STRUCTURE/
    MEANING
    RED WALL

    newspaper

Find the compound word on the Red Wall with a beginning sound /n/, a middle sound /z/ made with an **s**, an ending sound /er/, and which names something delivered to your house to read.

15. PHONICS/MEANING
    BLUE WALL

    feathers

Find the word on the Blue Wall with a beginning sound /t/, a middle sound /TH/*, an ending sound /z/ made with an **s**, and which names what covers the body of a bird.

* /TH/ = voiced; /th/ = voiceless

16. PHONICS/MEANING
    WHITE WALL

    internet

Find the word on the White Wall that begins with a short /i/ sound, has a /ter/ sound in the middle, ends with the /net/ sound, and names the tool that computers use to communicate worldwide.

17. PHONICS/STRUCTURE/
    MEAMNG

    immense

Find the word on the Blue Wall with a beginning sound /ĭ/, a middle sound /m/ an ending sound /s/, and which means the same as the word *huge.*

18. PHONICS/MEANING
    RED WALL

    tunnel

Find the word on the Red Wall with a beginning sound /t/, a middle sound /n/, an ending sound /l/, and which names a big opening in a mountain through which we can drive.

19. PHONICS/MEANING
    WHITE WALL

    shave

Find a word on the White Wall with a beginning sound /sh/, a middle sound /ā/ because of a silent **e** at the end, an ending sound /v/, and which names what a man does with lather and a razor every morning.

20. STRUCTURE/MEANING
    RED WALL

    I've

Find the contraction for the two words *I have* on the Red Wall.

21. PHONICS/MEANING
    BLUE WALL

    erase

Find the word on the Blue Wall that begins with a long /e/ sound, has a long /ā/ sound in the middle, ends in an **s e** pattern, and means "to remove completely."

22. PHONICS/STRUCTURE/
MEANING
WHITE WALL

fixed

Find the word on the White Wall with a beginning sound /f/, an ending sound /t/ made with the **e d** pattern, and which means the same as *repaired.*

23. PHONICS/STRUCTURE/
MEANING
RED WALL

toughest

Find the word on the Red Wall with a beginning sound /t/, a middle sound /f/ made with a **g h** pattern, ending with the suffix **est**, and which means the strongest thing or person in a group.

24. PHONICS/MEANING
BLUE WALL

accident

Find the word on the Blue Wall with a beginning sound /ăk/ made with an **a c** pattern, a middle sound /s/ made with a **c**, an ending sound /t/, and which names a bad thing that does not happen on purpose.

25. PHONICS/CONTEXT
RED WALL

precision

Find the word on the Red Wall with a beginning sound /pr/, a middle sound /ĭ/, an ending sound /shən/ made with an **s i o n** pattern, and which fits into this sentence: The medical instruments used by surgeons allow them to operate with _____ .

. . . .

WORD LIST 4: SYNONYMS,

ANTONYMS, HOMONYMS

*T*he Word Wall is not intended to be the only curriculum tool used for vocabulary development. This purposeful limitation of its role in the classroom is nowhere more evident than in the teaching of difficult concepts such as synonyms, antonymns and homonyms. Students must, therefore, be provided with some instruction in these word classes and their function in the language before this list or any others you might develop are used.

Before *The Word Wall* is used the following basic concepts should be known to students: synonyms as words with the same or similar meanings; antonyms as words with the opposite or nearly opposite meanings; homonyms as words with the same sound or spelling but different meanings. Then, because of its game orientation, and its ability to present the same materials in different ways throughout the year, *The Word Wall* will provide the valuable instructional components of reinforcement and review.

Once your students have had the concepts introduced to them through classroom instruction and had those concepts anchored and established by the use of *The Word Wall*, vocabulary extension of these particular word classes becomes relatively easy to accomplish through the addition of other words in this class to *The Word Wall* and the development of lists that address these new words.

1. PHONICS/ANTONYM
   BLUE WALL

   forward

Find the word on the Blue Wall with a beginning sound /f/, a middle sound /w/, an ending sound /d/, and which is an antonym for the word *backward*.

2. PHONICS/SYNONYM
   ORANGE WALL

   crazy

Find the word on the Orange Wall with a beginning sound /kr/ made with a **c r** pattern, a middle sound /ā/, an ending sound of /zē/ made with a **z y** pattern, and which is a synonym for the word *nuts*.

3. PHONICS/HOMONYM
   RED WALL

   peak

Find the word on the Red Wall that names the top of a mountain, and which sounds exactly the same as the word spelled **p-e-e-k**.

4. PHONICS/SYNONYM
   BLUE WALL
   smile

Find the word on the Blue Wall with a beginning sound /sm/, a middle sound /ī/ because of a silent **e** at the end, an ending sound /l/, and which is a synonym for the word *grin*.

5. PHONICS/ANTONYM
   BLUE WALL

   inside

Find the compound word on the Blue Wall with a middle sound /s/, an ending sound /d/, and which is an antonym for the word *outside*.

6. PHONICS/HOMONYM/
   MEANING
   WHITE WALL

   beat

Find the word on the White Wall that names what you do to me when you win a race that we are running, and which sounds exactly the same as the word spelled **b-e-e-t**.

7. PHONICS/SYNONYM
   RED WALL

   allowed

Find the word on the Red Wall with the same beginning sound as the word *across*, a double l in the middle, an ending sound /d/, and which is a synonym for the word *permitted*.

8. PHONICS/ANTONYM
   ORANGE WALL

   true

Find the word on the Orange Wall with a beginning sound /tr/, the same ending vowel sound as the word *blue*, and which is an antonym for the word *false*.

9. PHONICS/SYNONYM
   BLUE WALL

   timid

Find the word on the Blue Wall with a beginning sound /t/, a middle sound /m/, an ending sound /d/, and which is a synonym for the word *shy*.

10. PHONICS/HOMONYM
    MEANING
    YELLOW WALL

    prey

Find the word on the Yellow Wall with a beginning sound /pr/, an ending sound /ā/ made with an **e y** pattern, and which is a homonym for the word **p-r-a-y**, and which names an animal hunted by other animals.

11. PHONICS/SYNONYM
    RED WALL

    scared

Find the word on the Red Wall with a beginning sound /sk/ made with an **s c** pattern, a middle sound /air/, an ending sound /d/, and which is a synonym for the word *frightened*.

12. PHONICS/STRUCTURE/
    ANTONYM
    WHITE WALL

    output

Find the compound word on the White Wall with the same beginning sound as the word *outside*, a middle sound /p/, an ending sound /t/, and which is an antonym for the word *input*.

13.	PHONICS/HOMONYM ORANGE WALL	Find the word on the Orange Wall with a beginning sound /s/, a middle sound /ē/ made with an **e a** pattern, an ending sound /m/, and which is a homonym for the word **s-e-e-m**.
	seam	

14.	PHONICS/SYNONYM BLUE WALL	Find the word on the Blue Wall with a beginning sound /g/, a middle sound /ō/, an ending sound /z/ made with an **s**, and which is a synonym for the word *leaves*.
	goes	

15.	PHONICS/ANTONYM RED WALL	Find the word on the Red Wall with a beginning sound /kw/ made with a **q u** pattern, with middle sounds /ī/ and /ə/, an ending sound /t/, and which is an antonym for the word *noisy*.
	quiet	

16.	PHONICS/HOMONYM BLUE WALL	Find the word on the Blue Wall with a beginning sound /gr/, a middle sound /ō/ made with an **o w** pattern, an ending sound /n/, and which is a homonym for the word **g-r-o-a-n**.
	grown	

17.	PHONICS/STRUCTURE/ ANTONYM WHITE WALL	Find the compound word on the White Wall with the same beginning sound as the word *if*, a middle sound /s/, an ending sound /d/, and which is an antonym for the word *outside*.
	inside	

18.	PHONICS/SYNONYM ORANGE WALL	Find the word on the Orange Wall with a beginning sound /h/, it rhymes with the word *vault*, and which is a synonym for the word *stop*.
	halt	

19. PHONICS/HOMONYM/
    MEANING
    RED WALL

    feat

Find the word on the Red Wall with a beginning sound /f/, a middle sound /ē/ made with an **e a** pattern, an ending sound /t/, and which means a brave act, and is a homonym for the word **f-e-e-t**.

20. PHONICS/SYNONYM
    BLUE WALL

    peril

Find the word on the Blue Wall with a beginning sound /p/, a middle sound /r/, an ending sound /l/, and which is a synonym for the word *danger*.

21. PHONICS/ANTONYM
    BLUE WALL

    closed

Find the word on the Blue Wall with a beginning sound /kl/, made with a **c l** pattern, a middle sound /ō/ because of a silent **e** at the end, an ending sound /d/, and which is an antonym for the word *open*.

22. PHONICS/HOMONYM
    WHITE WALL

    passed

Find the word on the White Wall with a beginning sound /p/, the same vowel sound as the word *has*, an ending sound /t/ made with an **e d** pattern, and which is a homonym for the word **p-a-s-t**.

23. PHONICS/STRUCTURE/
    SYNONYM
    ORANGE WALL

    wicked

Find a two syllable word on the Orange Wall with a beginning sound /w/, a middle sound /k/, an ending sound /d/, and which is a synonym for the word *evil*.

24. PHONICS/SYNONYM
    RED WALL

    abrasion

Find the word on the Red Wall with a beginning sound the same as the word *at*, a middle sound /ā/, an ending sound /shən/ made with an **s i o n** pattern, and which is a synonym for the word *cut*.

WORD LIST 5: WORD FORM CLASSES

This list is effective as one part of the instructional flow of related language lessons, although it can be used on its own for it provides an understanding of parts of speech — word form classes — that language textbooks often do not supply. Naturally, familiarity with word form classes is necessary, and at least one direct teaching experience related to each classification should precede the use of the word list.

Whole language enthusiasts will, with just cause perhaps, argue for the exclusion of this section. But one of the major tenets of *The Word Wall* is the intent to carry *The Word Wall* and its familiar, broadly based vocabulary throughout the school day, and I believe that justifies its inclusion.

1. PHONICS/CLASS/MEANING
   RED WALL

   guards

   Find a noun on the Red Wall with a beginning sound /g/, a middle sound /ar/, an ending sound /z/ made by an **s**, and which names people who protect other people or property.

2. PHONICS/CLASS/CONTEXT
   ORANGE WALL

   preheat

   Find a verb on the Orange Wall that begins with the prefix **pre**, a middle sound /h/, an ending sound /t/, and which fits into this sentence: Mom must _____ the oven before she puts in the cake.

3. PHONICS/CLASS/CONTEXT
   YELLOW WALL

   delicious

   Find the adjective on the Yellow Wall with a beginning sound /d/, a middle sound /sh/ made with a **c i** pattern, an ending sound /əs/, and which fits into this sentence: Dad's pizza always tastes _____.

4. PHONICS/CLASS/CONTEXT
   GREEN WALL

   quickly

   Find an adverb on the Green Wall with a beginning sound /kw/, a middle sound /k/ made with a **c k** pattern, an ending sound /lē/ made with an **l y** pattern, and which fits into this sentence: Victor can run very _____.

5. SIGHT/CLASS/CONTEXT
   BLUE WALL

   he

   Find a pronoun on the Blue Wall that will take the place of the name *George* in this sentence: George does not like ice cream.

6. PHONICS/CLASS/SYNONYM
   WHITE WALL

   foe

   Find a noun on the White Wall with the beginning sound /f/, it rhymes with the word *toe*, and is a synonym for the word *enemy*.

7. PHONICS/CLASS/CONTEXT
   ORANGE WALL

   scrape

   Find a verb on the Orange Wall with a beginning sound /skr/ made with an **s c r** pattern, a middle sound /ā/ because of a silent **e** at the end, a final sound /p/, and which fits into this sentence: Dad had to _____ off the old paint on the wall before he could paint it again.

8. PHONICS/CLASS/MEANING
   WHITE WALL

   croak

Find a verb on the White Wall with a beginning sound /kr/ made with a **c r** pattern, a middle sound /ō/ made with an **o a** pattern, an ending sound /k/, and which names the sound a frog makes.

9. PHONICS/CLASS/CONTEXT
   ORANGE WALL

   slowly

Find an adverb on the Orange Wall with a beginning sound /sl/, a middle sound /ō/ made with an **o w** pattern, an ending sound /lē/ made with an **l y** pattern, and which fits into this sentence: Because she walked so _____, she was late for the party.

10. SIGHT/CLASS/CONTEXT/
    MEANING
    RED WALL

    her

Find a pronoun on the Red Wall that will take the place of the word *Donna's* in this sentence: Heather wore Donna's dress to the party.

11. PHONICS/CLASS/MEANING
    WHITE WALL

    doughnut

Find a noun on the Blue Wall with a beginning sound a /d/, a silent **g h** in the middle, an ending sound /t/, and which names a cookie with a hole in the middle of it.

12. PHONICS/CLASS/MEANING
    RED WALL

    surround

Find a verb on the Red Wall with a beginng sound /s/, a middle sound /r/, an ending sound /d/, and which means to be on all sides of something at the same time.

13. PHONICS/CLASS/SYNONYM
    ORANGE WALL

    crazy

Find an adjective on the Orange Wall with a beginning sound /kr/ made with a **c r** pattern, a middle sound /ā/, an ending sound /zē/ made with a **z y** pattern, and which is a synonym for the word *nuts*.

14. PHONICS/CLASS/
    STRUCTURE/CONTEXT
    BLUE WALL

    carefully

Find an adverb on the Blue Wall with a beginning sound /k/ made by a **c**, with two suffixes, and which fits into this sentence: The boys and girls were told to cross the street very _____.

15. SIGHT/CLASS/CONTEXT
    ORANGE WALL

    she

Find the pronoun on the Orange Wall that will take the place of the name *Mary* in this sentence: Mary ate all of the chocolate cake by herself.

16. PHONICS/CLASS/MEANING
    WHITE WALL

    wonder

Find the verb on the White Wall with the beginning sound /w/, a middle sound /n/, an ending sound /dər) and which names what we do when we are confused about something.

17. PHONICS/CLASS/MEANING
    RED WALL

    diamonds

Find a plural noun on the Red Wall with a beginning sound /d/, a middle sound /m/, an ending sound /z/ made with an **s**, and which names very valuable, white stones.

18. PHONICS/CLASS/SYNONYM
    ORANGE WALL
    wicked

Find an adjective on the Orange Wall with a beginning sound /w/, a middle sound /k/, an ending sound /d/, and which means the same as the word *evil*.

19. PHONICS/CLASS/CONTEXT
    BLUE WALL

    poorly

Find the adverb on the Blue Wall with a beginning sound /p/, the same vowel sound as the word *door*, ending with the suffix **ly**, and which fits into this sentence: Jon did very _____ on his Math Test.

20. PHONICS/MEANING
    WHITE WALL

    program

Find the word on the White Wall that begins with the / p r / sound, has a long /ō/ sound in the middle, ends in an /m/ sound, and names both a kind of tv show and a computer application.

21. STRUCTURE/CLASS/
    MEANING
    WHITE WALL

    sailboat

Find the compound noun on the White Wall that names a boat which uses the wind for its power.

22. PHONICS/CLASS/SYNONYM
    RED WALL

    complete

Find the verb on the Red Wall with a beginning sound /k/ made with a c, with the same vowel sound as the word *seat*, an ending sound /t/, and which is a synonym for the word *finish*.

23. PHONICS/CLASS/ANTONYM
    WHITE WALL

    smooth

Find the adjective on the White Wall with a beginning sound /sm/, with the same ending sound as the word *soothe*, and which is an antonym for the word *rough*.

24. PHONICS/CLASS/MEANING
    ORANGE WALL

    quietly

Find the adverb on the Orange Wall with the beginning sound /kw/, with middle sounds /ī/ and /ĕ/, ending with the suffix **ly**, and which means the same as the word *silently*.

25. SIGHT/CLASS/CONTEXT
    BLUE WALL

    it

Find the pronoun on the Blue Wall that will take the place of the words *the car* in this sentence: The car would not start.

WORD LIST 6: SURPRISE SOUNDS

Although many English words are predictably regular in their phonemic patterns as they relate to actual spellings, there are words in the language whose phonemes do not correlate exactly with their graphemic signals. For example, the **s** at the beginning of the words *sugar* and *sure* has a /sh/ sound; the **b** at the end of *comb* and the **h** at the beginning of *honor* has no sound at all.

For many students these language irregularities cause confusion and this list, although not exhaustive, exposes your students to some of these words and focuses their attention on words that do not fit regular phoneme/grapheme correspondences.

Once an awareness of this language attribute is established with students, you can construct word lists that deal with the same irregularities. Increased exposure to phoneme/grapheme irregularities helps students to master vocabulary items containing "surprise sounds."

1. PHONICS/MEANING
   GREEN WALL

   sugar

Find the word on the Green Wall with the beginning sound /sh/ made by the letter **s**, a middle sound /g/, an ending sound /er/, and which names something we add to food to make it sweet.

2. PHONICS/MEANING
   WHITE WALL

   gnaw

Find the word on the White Wall beginning with a silent **g**, ending with the same sound as the word *saw*, and which names what a mouse does when it chews through a box of cereal.

3. PHONICS/MEANING
   RED WALL

   tongue

Find the word on the Red Wall with the beginning sound /t/, the ending sound /ng/ followed by silent **u e**, and which names the part of our body that tastes food.

4. PHONICS/MEANING
   YELLOW WALL

   frontier

Find the word on the Yellow Wall with the beginning sound /fr/, a middle sound /ŭ/ made by the letter **o**, ending with the same sound as the word *spear*, and which names new and unexplored places.

5. PHONICS/MEANING
   ORANGE WALL

   opaque

Find the word on the Orange Wall with the beginning sound /ō/, a middle sound /ā/, an ending sound /k/ made by the pattern **q-u-e**, and which means not able to be seen through.

6. PHONICS/MEANING
   BLUE WALL

   honest

Find the word on the Blue Wall beginning with a silent **h**, a middle sound /n/, an ending sound /t/, and which names what we call people who never cheat, lie, or steal.

7. PHONICS/MEANING
   GREEN WALL

   campaign

Find the word on the Green Wall with a beginning sound /k/ made with a **c**, a middle sound /p/, ending with the pattern **p a i g n** that sounds like the word *pain* and which means an organized activity for a planned purpose.

43

8. PHONICS/MEANING
   YELLOW WALL

   fatigue

Find the word on the Yellow Wall with a beginning sound /f/, a middle sound /t/, an ending sound /g/, followed by silent **u e**, and which means very tired.

9. PHONICS/MEANING
   WHITE WALL

   league

Find the word on the White Wall with a beginning sound /l/, an ending sound /g/, followed by silent **u e**, and which completes the name of this group of teams: National Football _____.

10. PHONICS/MEANING
    ORANGE WALL

    initial

Find the word on the Orange Wall with a beginning sound / ĭ/, a middle sound / ĭ/, an ending sound /əl/, and which names the first letter of your name.

11. PHONICS/MEANING
    RED WALL

    insure

Find the word on the Red Wall with a beginning sound / ĭ/, a middle sound /sh/ made with an **s**, an ending sound /r/ followed by a silent **e**, and which means to guard against bad things happening.

12. PHONICS/MEANING
    GREEN WALL

    influential

Find the word on the Green Wall with the beginning sound / ĭ/, a middle sound /ū/, an ending sound /shəl/ made with the pattern **t i a l**, and which means to have great effect on someone or something.

13. PHONICS/MEANING
    YELLOW WALL

    grotesque

Find the word on the Yellow Wall with the beginning sound /gr/, a middle sound /t/, an ending sound of /k/ made by the pattern **q u e**, and which means huge and ugly.

14. PHONICS/MEANING
    WHITE WALL

    nausea

Find the word on the White Wall with a beginning sound /n/, a middle sound /s/, ending with a vowel pair in which both vowels are heard, and which means to be sick to your stomach.

15. PHONICS/MEANING
    BLUE WALL

    region

Find the word on the Blue Wall with the beginning sound /r/, a middle sound /j/, made with the pattern **g i**, ending with the same sound as the ending sound of the word *onion* and which means the same thing as special place or area.

16. PHONICS/MEANING
    YELLOW WALL

    aisle

Find the word on the Yellow Wall with the beginning sound /ī/ made by the pattern **a i**, a silent **s** in the middle, an ending sound of /l/, and which names the passage between desks or rows of seats.

17. PHONICS/MEANING
    RED WALL

    superficial

Find the word on the Red Wall with the beginning sound /s/, a middle sound /f/, ending with the pattern **c i a l**, and which means not very deep.

18. PHONICS/MEANING
    GREEN WALL

    hypochondria

Find the word on the Green Wall with a beginning sound /hī/ made with the pattern **h y**, a middle sound /k/ made by the pattern **c h**, ending with a vowel pair in which both vowels are heard, and which describes a person who constantly believes he's sick even though he is not.

19. PHONICS/MEANING
    BLUE WALL

    inertia

Find the word on the Blue Wall with a beginning sound /ĭ/, a middle sound /er/, an ending sound /shə/ made with the pattern **t i a**, and which names a scientific principle.

20. SIGHT/MEANING
    WHITE WALL

    hors d'oeuvre

Find the words on the White Wall that names small snacks served before dinner or at parties.

WORD LIST 7: WORDS
THAT CHALLENGE

No classroom, regardless of its socio-economic environment or surrounding school structure, is ever composed of students who are truly homogenously grouped by ability. Provisions must therefore be made for all learners wherever their abilities to happen to fall on the scope and sequence charts.

The word lists presented earlier were designed with this classroom reality in mind. They provide the raw materials of vocabulary acquisition in a developmental and spirally reinforced manner, and they were targeted toward mastery of the kinds of words included here and in the eighth word list. These "hard words" for elementary school students are intended to serve as both goad and goal. For the less capable student they provide a tangible goal toward which they can aim; for more able students they give significance, direction, and extension to the program.

These lists, and similar ones you construct during the latter half of the school year, are where *The Word Wall* was intended to take your students. More confident and aware of the language through many past exposures to *The Word Wall* (and collateral materials), learners find these lists to be stretching exercises that will open up their minds and provide them with two of the most essential tools they need to further their educations — a strong and broadly based operational awareness of the language, and the beginnings of a powerful vocabulary.

1. PHONICS/MEANING
   GREEN WALL

   bravado

Find the word on the Green Wall with the beginning sound /br/, a middle sound, /ă/, an ending sound /ō/, and which means make believe courage.

2. PHONICS MEANING
   RED WALL

   emancipate

Find the word on the Red Wall with a beginning sound /ē/, a middle sound /s/ made with a **c i** pattern, an ending sound /t/, and which means to set free.

3. PHONICS/MEANING
   YELLOW WALL

   elaborate

Find the word on the Yellow Wall with a beginning sound /ē/, a middle sound /b/, an ending sound /t/, and which means very fancy.

4. PHONICS/MEANING
   BLUE WALL

   pittance

Find the word on the Blue Wall with the beginning sound /p/, a middle sound of /t/, an ending sound /s/ made with a **c**, and which means a very small amount of money.

5. PHONICS/MEANING
   ORANGE WALL

   prohibition

Find the word on the Orange Wall with the beginning sound /prō/, the middle sounds /h ĭ/ and /bĭsh/, an ending sound /ən/, and which means to forbid something to happen.

6. PHONICS/MEANING
   WHITE WALL

   sustenance

Find the word on the White Wall with the beginning sound /s/, the name of the number ten in the middle, an ending sound /s/ made by **c**, and which names the foods we need to stay alive.

7. PHONICS/STRUCTURE/
   ANTONYM
   GREEN WALL

   unproductive

Find the word on Green Wall beginning with the prefix **un**, a middle sound /d/, an ending sound /v/, and which is the antonym for the word *productive*.

8. PHONICS/MEANING
   YELLOW WALL

   reminiscent

Find the word on the Yellow Wall with the beginning sound /r/, a middle sound /n/, an ending sound made by the other name for a *penny*, and which means to remember the good things about the past.

9. PHONICS/MEANING
   GREEN WALL

   litigate

Find the word on the Green Wall with a beginning sound /l/, a middle sound / ĭ/, an ending sound /t/, and which means to allow lawyers and judges to solve problems.

10. PHONICS/MEANING
    RED WALL

    ingenuity

Find the word on the Red Wall with the beginning sound / ĭ/, a middle sound /j/ made with a **g e** pattern, an ending sound /tē/ made with a **t y** pattern, and which means cleverness.

11. PHONICS/MEANING
    GREEN WALL

    dilapidated

Find the word on the Green Wall with a beginning sound /d/, a middle sound /p/, an ending sound /d/, and which means shabby and run-down.

12. SIGHT/MEANING
    WHITE WALL

    spontaneous

The word *spontaneous* means without planning. Find the word *spontaneous* on the White Wall.

13. PHONICS/MEANING
    ORANGE WALL

    severity

Find the word on the Orange Wall with a beginning sound /s/, a middle sound /v/, an ending sound /tē/ made with a **t y** pattern, and a meaning which comes from the root [base] word *severe*.

14. SIGHT/MEANING
    BLUE WALL

    relinquish

Find the word on the Blue Wall spelled **r-e-l-i-n-q-u-i-s-h**, pronounced /rĭ-**lĭng**-kwĭsh/, and which means to give up something to another.

15. PHONICS/STRUCTURE/
    MEANING
    GREEN WALL
    rehabilitate

Find the word on Green Wall that begins with the prefix **re**, has a middle sound /b/, an ending sound /t/, and which means to return a person to his original state of goodness.

16. PHONICS/STRUCTURE/
    MEANING
    WHITE WALL

    pacification

Find the word on the White Wall with a beginning sound /p/, a middle sound /f/, ending with the suffix **tion**, and which means to make peaceful.

17. SIGHT/MEANING
    ORANGE WALL

    optimism

Find the word on the Orange Wall that says *optimism* and which means to always look at the good side of things.

18. PHONICS/MEANING
    BLUE WALL

    obscurity

Find the word on the Blue Wall with a beginning sound /ŏb/, a middle sound /skyoor/, an ending sound /tē/ made with a **t y** pattern, and which means not easy to understand.

19. PHONICS/MEANING
    GREEN WALL

    generosity

Find the word on Green Wall with the beginning sound /j/ made with a **g**, a middle sound /er/, an ending sound /tē/ made with a **t y** pattern, and which comes from the root [base] word *generous*.

20. PHONICS/STRUCTURE/
    MEANING
    RED WALL

    misrepresentation

Find the word on the Red Wall that begins with the prefix **mis**, ends with the suffix **tion**, and which comes from the root [base] word *represent*.

21. SIGHT/MEANING
ORANGE WALL

premeditate

Find the word on the Orange Wall that says *premeditate*, and which means to think about in advance.

22. PHONICS/STRUCTURE
MEANING
YELLOW WALL

ratification

Find the word on the Yellow Wall that is built upon the root [base] word *ratify*, ends with the suffix **tion**, and which means to accept laws by vote.

23. PHONICS/MEANING
GREEN WALL

stability

Find the word on the Green Wall with the beginning sound /st/, a middle sound /b/, an ending sound /tē/ made with a **t y** pattern, and which means something that does not change or move much.

24. PHONICS/MEANING
BLUE WALL

adolescence

Find the word on the Blue Wall with a beginning sound /ă/, a middle sound /l/, an ending sound /s/ made with a **c e** pattern, and which names the years between 12 and 18 in a human child.

25. PHONICS/MEANING
ORANGE WALL

anatomy

Find the word on the Orange Wall with a beginning sound /ă/, a middle sound /t/, an ending sound /ē/ made with a **y**, and which means the study of the human body.

WORD LIST 8: MORE WORDS

THAT CHALLENGE

1. PHONICS/CONTEXT
   GREEN WALL

   flourescent

   Find the word on the Green Wall with the beginning sound /fl/, a middle sound /rĕz/, an ending sound /sĕnt/, and which fits into this sentence: The lights in the room were _____.

2. SIGHT/SYNONYM
   YELLOW WALL
   policeman

   Find the compound word on the Yellow Wall that is a synonym for the word *cop*.

3. PHONICS/MEANING
   BLUE WALL

   remote

   Find the word on the Blue Wall with the beginning sound /re/, a middle sound /ō/, because of a silent **e** at the end, an ending sound /t/, and which means far away from.

4. PHONICS/MEANING
   YELLOW WALL

   bacteria

   Find the word on the Yellow Wall with the beginning sound /b/, a middle sound that rhymes with *gear*, a double vowel ending sound of /ē/ and /ă/, and which names tiny animals that cause illness.

5. PHONICS/MEANING/
   STRUCTURE
   GREEN WALL

   preheat

Find the word on the Green Wall that begins with the prefix **pre**, a middle sound /h/, and an ending sound /t/, and which means the same as to warm up.

6. PHONICS/MEANING
   WHITE WALL

   sequence

Find the word on the White Wall with the beginning sound /s/, a middle sound /kw/, an ending sound /s/ made with a **c e** pattern and which means to happen in a certain order.

7. PHONICS/MEANING
   YELLOW WALL

   nomadic

Find the word on the Yellow Wall with the beginning sound /n/, a middle sound /ă/, an ending sound /k/ made with a **c**, and which means wandering from place to place with no real destination in mind.

8. PHONICS/MEANING
   BLUE WALL

   intricate

Find the word on the Blue Wall with a beginning sound /ĭn/, a middle sound /trə/, an ending sound /t/, and which means very complicated.

9. PHONICS/MEANING
   YELLOW WALL

   library

Find the word on the Yellow Wall with a beginning sound /l/, a middle sound /br/, an ending sound /ē/ made with a **y**, and which names the place we go to borrow books.

10. PHONICS/MEANING
    WHITE WALL

    fiction

Find the word on the White Wall with the beginning sound /f/, a middle sound /k/ made with a **c**, an ending sound /shən/ made with a **t i o n** pattern, and which names a story that is not true.

11. PHONICS/MEANING
YELLOW WALL

docile

Find the word on the Yellow Wall with the beginning sound /d/, a middle sound /s/ made with a **c**, an ending sound /l/, and which means quiet and easy to control.

12. PHONICS/MEANING
GREEN WALL

alternatives

Find the word on the Green Wall with a beginning sound /all/, a middle sound /ter/, an ending sound /z/ made with an **s**, and which is a synonym for the word *choices*.

13. SIGHT/ANTONYM
ORANGE WALL

opaque

Find the word on the Blue Wall with a beginning sound /ō/, and which is an antonym for the word *transparent*.

14. PHONICS/SYNONYM
GREEN WALL

complete

Find the word on the Green Wall with a beginning sound /k/ made with a **c**, a middle sound /pl/, an ending sound /t/, and which is a synonym for the word *finish*.

15. PHONICS/MEANING
YELLOW WALL

carp

Find the word on the Yellow wall that rhymes with *tarp*, and which names a kind of fish.

16. PHONICS/SYNONYM
WHITE WALL

frighten

Find the word on the White Wall with the beginning sound /fr/, a silent **g h** in the middle, an ending sound /n/, and which is a synonym for the word *scare*.

17. PHONICS/MEANING/
STRUCTURE
BLUE WALL

crossroads

Find the compound word on the Blue Wall with the beginning sound /kr/ with a **c r** pattern, a middle sound /r/, an ending sound /z/ made with an **s**, and which names a place where two roads cross.

18. PHONICS/MEANING ORANGE WALL invisible	Find the word on the Orange Wall that begins with the prefix **in**, a middle sound /v/, an ending sound /bəl/, made with the **b l e** pattern, and which means not able to be seen.
19. PHONICS/MEANING YELLOW WALL constant	Find the word on the Yellow Wall with the beginning sound /k/ made with a **c**, a middle sound /st/, an ending sound /t/, and which means never changing.
20. PHONICS/SYNONYM GREEN WALL attorney	Find the word on the Green Wall with the beginning sound /ă/, a middle sound /ter/, an ending sound /ē/ made with an **e y** pattern, and which is a synonym for the word **lawyer**.
21. PHONICS/MEANING YELLOW WALL encode	Find the word on the Yellow Wall with the beginning sound /ĕn/, a middle sound /k/ made with a **c**, an ending sound /d/, and which means to put into code.
22. PHONICS/ANTONYM ORANGE WALL external	Find the word on the Orange Wall with the beginning sound /ĕks/ made with an **e x** pattern, a middle sound /ter/, an ending sound /l/, and which is an antonym for the word *internal*.
23. PHONICS/ANTONYM GREEN WALL opinion	Find the word on the Green Wall with the beginning sound /ō/, a middle sound /p/, an ending sound /n/, and which is an antonym for the word *fact*.

24. PHONICS/MEANING
YELLOW WALL

barometer

Find the word on the Yellow Wall with the beginning sound /b/, a middle sound /rŏm/, an ending sound /er/, and which names a tool used to forecast the weather.

25. PHONICS/MEANING/
ORANGE WALL

revenge

Find the word on the Orange Wall with the beginning sound /r/, a middle sound /v/, an ending sound /j/ sound made by a **g**, and which means to get back at someone for hurting you.

. . . .

REINFORCEMENT AND

EVALUATION

The primary goal of *The Word Wall* is to extend and expand students' vocabulary, but it alone cannot assume the total responsibility for retention and application. Reinforcement and follow-up activities must also be utilized if what is introduced and practised during the *The Word Wall* game is to be of continuing value to your students.

The range of possible activities that will assist this objective of the program is extremely broad and, as was noted earlier, will not always appear as formalized curricula. Students will, on their own, often use *The Word Wall* as a spell-check program or thesaurus during writing assignments and as a general resource during other language related activities. This informal use of *The Word Wall* in other than the game setting is of great value and should be encouraged. However, the activities that follow are also a necessary component of the program. All of them have been used for reinforcement and evaluation; all are constructed with the intent of challenging the students' command of vocabulary taught through *The Word Wall*. Such activities are most effective when used as a natural part of an instructional cycle in which the words chosen for the game phase are then recycled throughout the following week in a variety of formats. Their effectiveness is enhanced when they are not confined to one curriculum area. The more *The Word Wall* can cross the curriculum, the more likely your students' vocabulary will increase.

Vocabulary that can apply to different curriculum areas has not been included here for the obvious reason that its application varies, but the activity formats provided here are those that have been field tested over many years and proved themselves effective in all curriculum areas.

. . . .

REINFORCEMENT AND

EVALUATION ACTIVITIES :

FORMATS

1. Closure Paragraphs

First, read the story below and think of words that might fit the blanks. Then reread, and write the word that fits using a word from the wall color named under each blank.

The man who owned the _____ shop and made the best

WHITE WALL

cream puffs in the city thought that the _____ old man,

GREEN WALL

who had not eaten for days, was very _____ to refuse

ORANGE WALL

the free doughnuts he was offered if he left the front of the doughnut man's shop.

"All your _____ in front of my store is driving away

WHITE WALL

_____." he said. "The doughnuts are free if you will

RED WALL

just go away. It is _____ of you to refuse free food when

RED WALL

you are hungry and then do what I want you to do anyway,"

he said to the old man who got on his _____ and

WHITE WALL

began to peddle away.

"That's very _____," said the old man, "but last
_{GREEN WALL}

_____ when I asked you for a jelly doughnut you
_{BLUE WALL}

wanted to give me a glass of _____ instead. Wasn't I
_{WHITE WALL}

just as _____ and hungry then?"
_{GREEN WALL}

"Do as you want." The owner answered. "Cut off your

_____ to spite your face. See if I care."
_{RED WALL}

"You make me _____." The old man said. "You are
_{BLUE WALL}

only _____ to me when it helps you. I would rather that
_{ORANGE WALL}

you always treated me badly."

Answers given in **boldface** below.

The man who owned the **doughnut** shop and made the best cream puffs in the city thought that the **poor/hungry** [*choice*] old man, who had not eaten for days, was very **foolish** to refuse the free doughnuts he was offered if he left the front of the doughnut man's shop.

"All your **junk** in front of my store is driving away **business**," he said. "The doughnuts are free if you will just go away. It is **dumb** of you to refuse free food when you are hungry and then do what I want you to do anyway," he said to the old man who got on to his **bicycle** and began to peddle away.

"That's very **funny**," said the old man, "but last **March** when I asked you for a jelly doughnut you wanted to give me a glass of **milk** instead. Wasn't I just as **poor** and hungry then?"

"Do as you want," the owner answered. "Cut off your **nose** to spite your face. See if I care."

"You make me **laugh**," the old man said. "You are only **kind** to me when it helps you. I would rather that you always treated me badly."

#2 – Contextual Sentences

Using a word from the wall color named under each blank, write the word that fits each sentence.

1. After he slipped and fell, Tony moved very _____.
_{ORANGE WALL}

2. When the thief broke into the woman's house, he stole her

   _____.
   RED WALL
3. The cop dunked his sugar _____ into his coffee
   WHITE WALL

   to soften it.
4. Ashley was _____ not to study for her test.
   ORANGE WALL

5. By the time we sat down for our late dinner, we were all

   very _____.
   GREEN WALL
6. Dad piled all the _____ in the pick-up truck to take
   WHITE WALL

   to the city dump.
7. Daniel could not go riding with his friends because the front

   wheel on his _____ was broken.
   WHITE WALL
8. My uncle's jokes are so _____ they make the whole
   GREEN WALL

   family laugh.
9. One of Tom's favorite _____ is to build model
   RED WALL

   airplanes.
10. The _____ at the circus was able to keep ten balls
    RED WALL

    balls in the air at the same time.

Answers
   1. slowly
   2. diamonds
   3. doughnut
   4. foolish/crazy [choice]
   5. hungry
   6. junk
   7. bicycle
   8. funny
   9. hobbies
  10. juggler

#3 - Better Word Exercise

In place of the word in CAPITALS in each sentence, write the word that fits from the wall color named.

1. Mom put the KITTEN full of water on the stove to heat.

   BLUE WALL: _____
2. January, February and MAY are the first three months of the year.

   BLUE WALL: _____
3. I helped my Dad ERASE the nails into the boards.

   RED WALL: _____
4. My aunt does very HAIRY things for the people she likes.

   ORANGE WALL: _____
5. When my cousin tells me a silly joke, I WALK until my sides hurt.

   BLUE WALL: _____
6. Terry put chocolate syrup into his CAR and drank it.

   WHITE WALL: _____
7. The little boy printed out a BANANA of his school project to hand in to his teacher.

   YELLOW WALL: _____
8. The RICH family that lived down the street from us never had enough to eat.

   GREEN WALL: _____
9. The stone sank quickly to the SIDE of the pond.

   BLUE WALL: _____
10. After the accident there was a POTATO in the fender of Dad's car.

    WHITE WALL: _____

Note: Using purposely silly items in some instances and straightforward ones in others, this activity is aimed as much at thinking skills and the experiential background of students as it is at developing vocabulary skills. The ability to recognize inconsistencies in what is read is a significant contributor to the development of vocabulary.

Answers:
1. kettle
2. March
3. pound
4. kind
5. laugh
6. milk
7. hardcopy
8. poor
9. bottom
10. dent

#4 - Analogies

In each of the items below there are two capitalized words that go together in a special way. They can be antonyms or synonyms. They can each be part of a whole, or they can show a difference in size. They can show different points in a sequence or they can tell something of the two words' spelling patterns.

Decide why the first two words go together. Now find a word from the wall color that fits with the third word in capitals.

Example: TIP is to SPEAR as ___POINT___ is to PENCIL.
(RED WALL)

A TIP is the sharp end of a SPEAR and a POINT is the sharp end of a PENCIL.

1. BRANCHES are to TRUNK as HEAD is to _____ .
GREEN WALL

2. FAST is to SLOW as WRITE is to _____ .
BLUE WALL

3. FAST is to SLOW as SMART is to _____ .
RED WALL

4. HIGH is to LOW as WISE is to _____ .
ORANGE WALL

5. GALLON is to QUART as DOLLAR is to _____ .
YELLOW WALL

6. MAN is to SKIN as FISH is to _____ .
YELLOW WALL

7. MEAT is to CARNIVORE as PLANTS are to _____ .
YELLOW WALL

8. RUDENESS is to INSULT as MANNERS is to _____ .
ORANGE WALL

62

9. PATIENT is to DOCTOR as CRIMINAL is to _____ .
   GREEN WALL

10. TINY is to HUGE as MIDGET is to _____ .
    GREEN WALL

This activity is an extremely powerful vocabulary builder once the fear of its intimidating form is overcome. It also attempts to meld reading and thinking skills. This format when preceded by the use of *The Word Wall* eases children into the development of skills that will later cause them to make such connections on their own, thus helping them to stretch their vocabulary base without the need for formal exercises.

Answers

1. neck
2. erase
3. dumb
4. foolish
5. quarters
6. scale
7. herbivore
8. apology
9. policeman
10. giant

#5 - Multiple Meanings

The same word fits each pair of sentences. Find the word on the wall color named and write it on the blank in each sentence.

1. WHITE WALL Dad does not like to _____ face every morning.
   "That was a close _____." Tom said after the speeding car just missed him.

2. GREEN WALL Mom told a _____ story at dinner last night and we all laughed.
   Terry told his mom that he couldn't go to school that day because his stomach felt _____.

3. RED WALL He had lost only one _____ after three weeks on a diet.

   My dad asked me to help him _____ out a dent in the fender of his car.

4. ORANGE WALL Laura's mom is a very _____ lady who does nice things for everyone.

   I don't like that _____ of candy.

5. WHITE WALL Frederick did not like to drink _____.

   The scientist was very careful when he tried to _____ the rattlesnake of its poison.

6. RED WALL George lit the _____ on the firecracker and threw it far away from him.

   The heat of a house fire will often _____ metal pipes together

7. RED WALL "You still don't get the _____!" Uncle John yelled at Dad.

   "Put a new _____ on your pencil," the teacher told Paul.

8. YELLOW WALL That small yellow fish is called a _____.

   Don't _____ on the same problem all the time.

9. WHITE WALL The sun's rays _____ down on the tin roof.

   Tom _____ the eggs until the white and yolk were well mixed.

10. YELLOW WALL The doctor used a set of _____ to weigh the baby.

    Dad removed the loose _____ and bones from the fish before he cooked it.

Note: Multiple meanings can confuse and confound students. This activity format, where difference in meaning depends upon context, helps students to increase their understanding of words with multiple meanings.

Answers

1. shave
2. funny
3. pound
4. kind
5. milk
6. fuse
7. point
8. carp
9. beat
10. scales

#6 - Antonyms

The word in capitals in each sentence is an antonym of the word that fits the sentence. Find the word that fits on the word wall named and write it above the word in capitals. Cross out the word in capitals.

black

Example: It was as ~~WHITE~~ as night in the cave. GREEN WALL

1. The SMALL distance between Earth and the moon does not frighten the astronauts. BLUE WALL

2. My father DESTROYED my bike so that I could ride it to school again. WHITE WALL

3. The doctor worked with great CLUMSINESS during the delicate operation. RED WALL

4. The CRIMINAL arrested the bank robber and took him to jail. YELLOW WALL

5. A NON-FICTION story is completely made up by the writer. WHITE WALL

6. His mother told him to play baseball INSIDE the house. BLUE WALL

7. The coach wanted his batters to run SLOWLY around the bases after they hit the ball. GREEN WALL

8. His teacher told him to work CARELESSLY through each math problem. BLUE WALL

9. The witch who did all those evil things was very KIND. ORANGE WALL

10. Because he did so WELL on his feet he got an F. BLUE WALL

Use this activity type with other words. Synonyms can be substituted for antonyms as shown by the next activity. A thinking component can be added by choosing not to use the capitalization clue and instructing students to find and correct the misplaced word on their own.

Answers

1. immense
2. fixed
3. precision
4. policeman
5. fiction
6. outside
7. quickly
8. carefully
9. wicked
10. poorly

 # 7 - Synonyms

The word in capitals in each sentence is a synonym of the word that fits the sentence. Find the word that fits on the word wall named, and write it above the word in capitals. Cross out the word in capitals.

huge
Example: The elephant was ~~ENORMOUS~~. RED WALL

1. Pete was a TRUTHFUL man. BLUE WALL

2. He could not REMEMBER the man's name. RED WALL

3. The witch's face was extremely EVIL looking. BLUE WALL

4. We will DEFEAT the Roosevelt Lions in the kickball game on Friday. WHITE WALL

5. He spent an extremely PLEASANT weekend with his cousin. WHITE WALL

6. Taylor got his first TWO-WHEELER when he was five years old. WHITE WALL

7. Dinosaurs were HUGE reptiles. BLUE WALL

8. He REPAIRED my bicycle for me in only two hours. WHITE WALL

9. The COP arrested the burglar. YELLOW WALL

10. I will KNOW her when we meet at the station. YELLOW WALL

Answers

1. honest
2. recall
3. sinister
4. beat
5. delightful
6. bicycle
7. immense
8. fixed
9. policeman
10. recognize

#8 – *Journal Activities*

Note: As in 1, all activities can be based on *any* word wall color.

1. Using only the WHITE (GREEN, YELLOW, BLUE, ORANGE, RED) WALL, write a short paragraph about someone you like very much. Ten of the words you use must be from the WHITE (GREEN, YELLOW, BLUE, ORANGE, RED) WALL. Underline the words used from the WALL.

2. Using only the GREEN WALL, write no more than a fifty-word paragraph that tells about your favorite TV show. Ten of the words in your paragraph must be from the GREEN WALL. Underline the words used from the WALL.

3. You have been set down on a strange new planet beyond Pluto. It is called Ramat. Using words from the RED WALL tell us about this planet you are on. Ten of the words you use must be from the RED WALL. Underline the words used from the WALL.

4. You have been granted three wishes by a magical genie. Using words from the BLUE WALL tell about what three wishes you would ask for and why you would ask for these things. Fifteen of the words you use must be from the BLUE WALL. Underline the words used from the WALL.

These writing activities will help you to judge growth among your students. Use this type of activity once every two weeks. Any topic is suitable as long as students are restricted to one color wall as their source.

Conclusion
All of the materials included here have been used successfully with student groups and are, therefore, ready to use. They are, however, only examples and do not exhaust all possibilities. The size of this work would be prohibitive if all past uses were included. Once *The Word Wall* is up and being used routinely as part of the classroom curriculum other applications will quickly become evident.

SPEED DRILL

Flash cards have always been a part of reading instruction in the elementary grades. When the look-and-say reading method was in favor, they were the mainstay of instruction. Even when the experts told us that the phonic elements of language instruction were of greater primary importance, they still held a curious, though secondary, draw for teachers of reading. Speed Drill is an extension of educators' perennial addiction to flash cards and it is also fun and challenging.

The object of Speed drill is to build upon students' existing sight vocabulary in much the same way that flash cards do, but within a game context that utilizes both competitiveness and personal goals in the process. For many students it provides a rarity in education — tangible results. Students see their competency grow throughout the school year as they add more words to their scores: because of observable growth they feel a true sense of improvement.

Students should be given the opportunity to play it once a month.

Rules for Speed Drill

Materials Needed

Word Wall
Stop watch or analog with sweep second hand for Timer
Pointer for Leader
Scorecard or plain white 5 X 7 inch index card for Scorer

Each round requires four participants. They are identified as:

Leader: This role is initially yours (the teacher's) until all students are acquainted with the procedures. It can then be filled by a student who can pronounce all the words to be used.

Reader: The student who reads the words as they are pointed out by the leader.

Timer: The student who starts, stops, and times the round.

Scorer: The student who counts and records the number of words correctly pronounced by the Reader.

Reader, Timer, and Scorer roles rotate until all participants have played each part.

Each round proceeds in the following manner.

1. The Leader chooses the three participants for the game and provides them with the materials they need.

2. The Reader says each of the words pointed to by the Leader as quickly and as clearly as he/she can.

3. The Timer begins with the word *start* and ends with the word *stop* spoken clearly paying strict attention to the timing device. (One minute is the usual time allotment.)

4. The Scorer adds check/tick-marks to the score card of the Reader each time the Leader says yes. No mark is made if the Leader pronounces the word for the Reader.

. . . .

AFTERWORD

This is the point in my book at which observations concerning the process might be natural, with the result that the next few pages could well (and naturally) be filled with statistics and arguments justifying the activity and aimed at convincing the reader that the time so far invested in reading these pages has not been wasted. But your time is not at issue here; rather it is the time of the target audience, the students, which is significant, and that is why I have chosen this way to end my book.

"Don't tell me what you think it is I want to hear," I told them, "tell me what you actually think of *The Word Wall*." Their responses follow:

"It makes us think."
> — Albert L., grade 4

"I like *The Word Wall* because it makes us think."
> — Jason D, grade 4

"I like *The Word Wall* because it helps us to pronounce words."
> — Randolf B., grade 5

"It gives you new words you never heard of."
> — Cassie H., grade 5

"It gets you to know new definitions of words."
> — Mauricio G., grade 5

"It helps you to read and spell better."
> — Claudia G., grade 5

"I like the game because it makes me feel happy."
> — Perla V., grade 4

"Some words are just too easy."
> — Tayari R., grade 5

"The first thing I like is that it gives our minds a time for thinking."

— Jerry N., grade 5

"We add words to our vocabulary."

— Camille C., grade 4

"*The Word Wall* is fun because you get to learn about new words."

— Diane A., grade 5

"You know more words when it is finished."

— Julio M., grade 3

"I like *The Word Wall* because you know how to say the word and you know its meaning."
— Nelson H., grade 5

"When it is tied and you know the word you feel like a hero."
— Duc C., grade 4

"Become a better reader."
— Garr T., grade 3

"It only comes once a week."
— Darryl T., grade 3

"It's fun to challenge the other team."
Joe W., grade 4

"We only play a short time."
— Bismark O., grade 5

"*The Word Wall* is fun and it makes us use your brains."
— Jason A., grade 6

"And last, but not least, we get ice cream at the end of the season."
— Michael S., grade 6

. . . .

APPENDIX A

Dolch's Thirteen Steps in Phonics Teaching

1. Single Consonants b c d f g h j k l m n p q r s t v y z
2. Consonant Digraphs ch sh th wh ph kn wr gn *blends
3. Short vowels a e i o u
4. Long vowels
5. Final **e** rule
6. Vowel Digraphs *Grp 1* al ay oa ea ei
                          Grp 2 au aw eu ew oo
7. Diphthongs ol oy ow
8. Vowels with r ar er ir or ur
9. Soft **c** and **g** c g
10. Prefix and Suffix un- re- non- dis- pro-
    -less -ness -able
    -tion -ly -ing -er- ful
11. Number of syllables
12. Division into syllables
13. Open or closed syllables

* These blends should also be taught:
  br cr dr fr gr pr tr
  bl cl fl gl pl sl sk sc sn sm sp ng
  st sw tw dw qu str scr spr spl thr

APPENDIX B

Consonants: Initial

b	— bat, big, baste, bite
c as /s/	— city, center, cite, cent
c as /k/	— carry, cup, cost
d	— dent, dust, deal
f	— for, fool, fuss
g as /g/	— goat, gun, gas
g as /j/	— giant, gem, gentle
h	— hold, heavy, horse
j	— jump, job, jerk
k	— kettle, kick, kid
l	— lamb, little, lose
m	— man, most, mayor
n	— nose, never, nice
p	— pose, punt, pucker
q as /kw/	— quick, quiet
r	— rent, rose, runt
s	— sell, sand, sorry
t	— tell, tamper, tuck
v	— vest, voyage, vent
w	— want, wonder, wick
x	— xerox, xylophone
y	— yellow, yell, yelp
z	— zebra, zinc, zipper

Consonants: Middle and End

b	— slab, mob, tab, sober
c as /s/	— pencil, princess, place, ace
c as /k/	— income, overcoat, epic, Vic

d	— maiden, indeed, lid, sod
f	— outfit, suffer, loaf, wife
g as /g/	— forget, again, vigor, rag
g as /j/	— magic, engine, forger, rage
h	— inhale, rehash, preheat
j	— major, injure, perjury
k	— market, make, beak
l	— sunlight, bullet, battle, bundle, bell
m	— apartment, armful, slam, crumb
n	— candle, dancing, brown, prune
p	— cupful, chipmunk, pipe, chip
q as /kw/	— require, inquire, request, bequest
q as /k/	— liquor, unique
r	— perfume, serve, shear, pleasure
s	— insult, result, grass, sense
t	— renter, platform, present, paste
v	— invite, saver, serve, envy
w	— highway, hardware
x as /ks/	— axes, boxes, fox, wax
z	— muzzle, buzz, fizz

Consonant Blends: Initial

bl	— blue, blame, bland
cl	— close, class, clown
fl	— flow, flake, flap
gl	— glow, glass, glimmer
pl	— plow, place, plate
sl	— slow, slim, slick
br	— brown, broke, breast
cr	— crown, crack, crumble
fr	— frown, free, fresh
gr	— grow, groan, grab
pr	— pray, proud, prowl
sc as /sk/	— scowl, scalp, scare
sc as /s/	— scent, scene, scenery
sk	— skate, sketch, skip
sm	— small, smell, smack
sn	— snow, sniff, snake
sp	— spot, spare, spike
st	— stone, stick, stem

sw	— swim, switch, swipe
tr	— train, trail, trip
tw	— twin, twine, twist
str	— straw, strap, strip
squ	— squeeze, squirm, squash
spl	— split, splice, splinter
scr	— scrap, scrape, scrub
spr	— spray, sprig, spring
thr	— through, threw, threat

Consonant Blends: Final

sk	— mask, task, whisk
st	— past, breakfast, waste
sp	— wasp, clasp, grasp
ck	— check, pick, slick

Ch, Th, Sh, Wh: Beginning

ch	— chunk, chart, chase
th as /th/	— thought, thick, thimble
th as /TH/	— them, though, they
sh	— shower, shake, shave
wh	— when, while, which

Ch, Th, Sh: Ending

ch	— such, which, bunch
th as /th/	— both, moth, filth
sh	— wash, sash, crash

The Schwa Sound

ə as in **a**bove
ə as in tak**e**n
ə as in penc**i**l
ə as in lem**o**n
ə as in cir**u**s

Vowel Dipthongs

ou	— bought, brought, fought
oy	— toy, boy, soy
oi	— oil, boil, soil, toil
ow as /ō/	— blow, sow, crow
ow	— plow, cow, meow
au	— taught, caught, fraught

Vowel Digraphs

ai as /ā/	— wait, pail, sail
ay as /ā/	— play, way, day
ew as /oo/	— flew, stew, crew
ea as /ē/	— plead, bean, steam
ea as ĕ	— head, bread, already
oo as /u /	— good, book, stood
oa as /ō/	— float, boat, coat

"r" Controlled Vowels

ar	— tar, star, bark
er as /er/	— never, over, serve
ir as /er/	— girl, stir, sir
or	— corner, forty, door
ur as /er/	— burn, curve, fur, purr

"y" as Vowel

y as /ē/	— icy, juicy
y as /ĭ/	— hymn
y as /ī/	— rye, sly

YELLOW WALL

carp

library

hardcopy

fatigue

docile

hundred

quarter

grotesque

nomadic

scales

barometer

herbivore

complete

relationship

constant

delicious

elaborate

ratification

recognize

enter

bacteria

reminiscent

encode

frontier

download

policeman

prey

aisle

ORANGE WALL

successful domesticate revenge

kind she

invisible

severity limestone

crazy

quality

apology

preheat

opaque

scrape

slowly

somersault anatomy

foolish

vigor true

premeditate

halt

initial

wicked

optimism

prohibition comfortable

seam quietly external

BLUE WALL

grown   doubt   region   relinquish

obscurity   feathers

pittance   March   adolescence

opportunity   he   cowboy

peril

inside   it   doubtful

sinister   grown

closed   goes

bottom

honest   smile

meat

immense

laugh

lung   timid   carefully

outside

intricate   accident

poorly   inertia

remote

forward   kettle

erase

WHITE WALL

sequence

defeat

delightful

wonder

passed

internet

smooth

inside

pacification

sailboat

frighten

spontaneous

foe

teacher

hors d'oeuvre

variable

nausea

sustenance

milk

league

crossroads

croak

bicycle

gnaw

doughnut

beat

program

dent

fixed

junk

fiction

output

shave

RED WALL

hobbies

newspaper

her

insure

tongue

abrasion

business

dumb

allowed

surround

misrepresentation

diamonds

point

superficial

toughest

nose

emancipate

matrix

juggler

I've

tunnel

feat

precision

ingenuity

peak

complete

huge

recall

pound

we've

quiet

guards

scared

fuse

GREEN WALL

burrow

rehabilitate

sugar

complete

bravado

opinion

attorney

hungry

stability

poor

campaign

funny

dilapidated

giant

reset

generosity

alternatives

smart

influential

quickly

inside

hypochondria

knowledge

litigate

flourescent

policeman

unproductive

neck

preheat